The Art of Finding Comfort and Joy:

Unleashing the Power of Hygge

By Maria Johanson

The Hygge Mindset: A Positive Approach to Life

As the pace of modern life speeds up, it's easy to feel overwhelmed, stressed, and anxious. But there is an antidote to this, a way of living that promotes coziness, comfort, and contentment. It's called the Hygge mindset, and it's a concept that originates from Denmark.

Hygge (pronounced hoo-gah) is difficult to translate, but it means something like "coziness" or "well-being." It's a philosophy of life that embraces simplicity, warmth, and contentment, and it's about creating a comfortable atmosphere that encourages relaxation and enjoyment.

The Hygge mindset is not just about creating a cozy home, although that is an essential part of it. It's also about finding joy in simple pleasures, connecting with loved ones, and taking care of yourself. It's about being present in the moment and enjoying the little things in life.

The Hygge mindset is an excellent antidote to stress and anxiety. It's a reminder that we don't need to have a lot of material possessions or achieve certain goals to be happy. Happiness can be found in small moments, like drinking a cup of hot chocolate by the fire or snuggling up with a loved one on the couch.

So how can you adopt the Hygge mindset in your everyday life? Here are a few ideas:

1. Create a cozy home.
Your home should be a sanctuary, a place where you feel safe and comfortable. To create a cozy home, focus on warmth, texture, and soft lighting. Add lots of blankets, pillows, and comfy chairs. Use warm colors and natural materials like wool, wood, and cashmere.

2. Enjoy simple pleasures.
Hygge is all about enjoying the little moments in life. Take a walk in the park, drink a cup of hot tea, enjoy a good book, or watch the sunset. It's the simple things that bring joy and peace.

3. Connect with loved ones.
Hygge is about creating a sense of community and connection. Spend time with family and friends, share a meal, play games, or have a movie night. Hygge is about enjoying the company of others and creating meaningful relationships.

4. Take care of yourself.

Self-care is essential to the Hygge mindset. Take a warm bath, practice yoga or meditation, or treat yourself to a spa day. Hygge is about embracing moments of relaxation and enjoying the little luxuries in life.

5. Embrace nature.

Nature is an essential part of the Hygge mindset. Take a walk in the woods, spend time gardening, or simply enjoy the beauty of nature. The natural world provides a sense of peace and tranquility that can help us feel more relaxed and content.

Adopting the Hygge mindset can help you find more joy and contentment in life. It's a reminder that happiness can be found in the small moments and that we don't need to have a lot of material possessions to be happy. So take a moment to breathe, relax, and enjoy the cozy comforts of life.

Embracing Simplicity: The Key to a Cozy Life

In a world that's constantly changing, it's easy to lose sight of what's important. With the never-ending demands of everyday life, it's easy to get caught up in the hustle and bustle and forget about the little things that truly matter. That's where simplicity comes in. Embracing the notion of simplicity isn't about giving up all your possessions or living like a monk, but rather about finding peace and contentment in the things that we already have. By living a simpler life, we can create a cozy and comforting environment around ourselves, leading to a happier and more fulfilling life.

Simplicity is not always a natural lifestyle choice as we live in a world bombarded by constant stimulation, materialism, and a "never enough" attitude, but it's a choice worth considering. When we detach ourselves from these influences and focus on the little things that matter, we begin to realize the true essence of living. A simpler life means we learn to enjoy the moment, stop to smell the roses, and appreciate the small things that bring joy and happiness to our lives.

One way to embrace simplicity is by focusing on decluttering our surroundings. The concept of minimalism is gaining popularity in recent times — in short, it is living with fewer possessions. It's about owning only what you need and love dearly, and nothing more. We often accumulate things we don't need or use, which can make life more complicated and cluttered. To start, begin by decluttering your home. Get rid of things that serve no purpose or bring no joy into your life. Start with one room, one corner or even one drawer. You can donate, sell, or even recycle items that no longer serve you.

By living in a decluttered space, we can easily manage things without feeling overwhelmed by physical and mental clutter. Cleaning becomes easier, preparing meals becomes more fun, and we don't have to worry about losing objects in piles of unmanageable clutter.

Another aspect of living a simple life is slowing down and appreciating the rhythms of life. Technology has made our lives easier, but it has also taken over too much of our time. It's important to disconnect sometimes, to turn off the phone, step back and recharge. Devoting even just a few hours a day to find calmness can be quite therapeutic; read a book, take a relaxing bath, take a walk in nature or cook a simple meal— it's amazing how the small things can bring contentment.

We sometimes miss out on experiences because of our constant need to be in control of our lives. By slowing down a bit, we can see things in a new light and appreciate the small, happy moments that we might otherwise overlook.

The concept of simplicity can also be applied to our relationships. By embracing and appreciating the people who share our lives, we can find that our relationships become stronger and more meaningful. Instead of rushing through conversations or taking each other for granted, we should step back and invest time into deeper, more meaningful connections.

Simplicity is quite often viewed as living with less, but it's instead about living with what's truly important. If we focus on what makes us happy and only allow those things into our lives, we can appreciate them more. This is seen in relationships too, for instance. We don't need to have several acquaintances in our social circle; instead, we can invest time and effort into a few, genuine friendships. This would help us build more meaningful relationships and understand what truly matters.

One other way to embrace simplicity is by being mindful of our consumption habits. We often consume mindlessly, buying things just for the sake of it. By being aware of our consumption habits and making more intentional choices, we can start to make a difference in the world. Supporting local businesses, shopping for less, eating less meat or even driving less can help reduce our carbon footprint, leading to a healthier, happier and more connected life.

In conclusion, embracing simplicity can help create a cozy and harmonious life. It's about living with what's truly important, focusing on the little things that can bring joy to our lives while taking the pressure off the things that don't. Simplicity is not about depriving oneself or living without basic necessities; rather, it's about being mindful of one's choices and prioritizing what's truly essential.

By revealing clutter, slowing down, choosing meaningful relationships, and being mindful of our consumption, we can lead a life that is more comforting, fulfilling, and enjoyable. Simplicity Saves us from the constant need to acquire more, allowing us to be happy with what we have while enjoying the peaceful environment we create. At times it may be hard, but it becomes easier once we start. You don't need to jettison your current life, but taking baby steps is often more attainable. Start by choosing just one thing to let go of and replace it with something that brings you joy. Soon, you'll realize that simplicity positively impacts every aspect of our lives, leading to a happier and more peaceful life.

The Power of Rituals: Finding Joy in the Mundane

Have you ever felt that your life has become a rut, and the days seem to blend together? Do you find yourself constantly looking for ways to add more meaning and purpose to your life, but somehow end up feeling unfulfilled? If so, you're not alone. Many of us struggle with the same feelings, trying to find our footing in a world that's constantly changing.

However, there's a simple yet effective answer to these problems- the power of rituals. By creating daily or weekly routines that we can look forward to, we can add a sense of joy and meaning to our lives.

Rituals may seem like a fancy word, but in reality, they're just habits we intentionally create. They can range from the simple, like making your bed every morning or enjoying a cup of tea before starting your day. Or they can be more complex, like taking a weekly dance class or hiking a new trail every weekend. Whatever the ritual may be, its intention is always the same- to create a meaningful and fulfilling experience that we can look forward to.

Rituals are not just about the actions we take, but the feelings they evoke within us. When we establish a ritual, we create a sense of stability and predictability in our lives. When we know what to expect, we can relax and let go of any unnecessary stress or worry. We become more present in the moment, allowing us to fully experience and appreciate what we're doing.

One example of a simple yet powerful ritual is creating a gratitude journal. In today's fast-paced world, we often focus on what we don't have instead of what we do. By taking a few minutes each day to write down three to five things we're grateful for, we can shift our perspective and focus on the positive aspects of our lives. This simple ritual can help us cultivate a sense of gratitude and contentment, boosting our mood and overall well-being.

Another example of a powerful ritual is setting aside time for self-care. Self-care rituals can range from a luxurious bubble bath to a morning yoga practice. Whatever self-care looks like for you, it's essential that you prioritize it in your life. By taking care of ourselves, we can better care for others and show up in our lives with more energy and presence.

One of my favorite rituals is cooking a meal with loved ones. Coming together to create a delicious meal not only satisfies our hunger but creates a sense of connection and togetherness. We can share stories, laugh, and bond over a shared experience. This ritual is not only nourishing for our bodies but also our souls.

Another example of the power of rituals is creating a morning routine. A morning ritual can set the tone for the entire day, helping us feel grounded, centered, and prepared for whatever comes our way. Whether it's taking a few deep breaths, meditating, or going for a morning run, a morning ritual can help us feel energized and ready to tackle the day ahead.

Incorporating rituals into our lives doesn't have to be complicated or time-consuming. It's about finding what works for you and intentionally creating habits that bring you joy and fulfillment. Rituals can be as simple or as complex as we want them to be, the key is to be consistent and intentional with them.

In conclusion, the power of rituals can transform the mundane into the meaningful. They can help us live more purposeful and fulfilling lives, creating a sense of joy and contentment that can't be found in the hustle and bustle of everyday life. By taking the time to intentionally create and prioritize rituals in our lives, we can cultivate a sense of stability, connection, and gratitude that will serve us in all areas of our lives.

So, what's your favorite ritual? How will you intentionally create more meaningful habits in your own life? Remember, the power is in your hands.

Cultivating Gratitude: The Art of Saying Thank You

Gratitude is a powerful emotion that can improve your life in many ways. It can make you happier, healthier, and more successful. Cultivating gratitude means learning to appreciate the people and things in your life and expressing your appreciation to others. Saying thank you is one of the simplest but most effective ways to show gratitude. In this chapter, we'll explore the art of saying thank you and how it can transform your life.

First, let's look at why gratitude is so important. Numerous studies have shown that practicing gratitude can improve your physical and mental health. It can reduce stress, lower blood pressure, improve sleep quality, and increase happiness. Gratitude can also improve your personal and professional relationships. When you express gratitude to others, they feel appreciated and valued, which strengthens your bond. Gratitude can even improve your career by making you more successful and productive.

So how do you cultivate gratitude? One of the easiest ways is to say thank you. This simple phrase can have a powerful impact on your life and the lives of those around you. Saying thank you shows that you appreciate what someone has done for you, whether it's a small or large gesture. It can also make the person feel good about themselves and encourage them to do more for others in the future.

Here are a few examples of how saying thank you can make a difference in your everyday life:

1. Thanking a coworker for their help on a project
If you work in an office, there are probably times when you need help from a co-worker to complete a project. When someone takes the time to assist you, make sure to thank them. It's easy to take help for granted, but acknowledging someone's efforts can make them feel valued and appreciated. Plus, the next time you need help, they'll be more likely to assist you again.

2. Thanking a friend for listening
When you're going through a tough time, it can be helpful to talk to a friend. Even if they can't solve your problems, just having someone to listen can make a big difference. Make sure to thank your friend for being there for you. They'll appreciate the recognition, and it will strengthen your friendship.

3. Thanking a family member for a small gesture
Small gestures can often have the biggest impact. Maybe your partner made you breakfast in bed or your mom sent you a care package in the mail. Whatever it is, make sure to

thank them for it. It shows that you appreciate the effort they put in to make your day a little brighter.

4. Thanking a stranger for their kindness
Sometimes, the person doing something kind for you is a complete stranger. Maybe they held the door open for you or let you merge in traffic. These small acts of kindness can make a big difference in your day. Take a moment to thank the person, and you'll both feel good about the interaction.

When it comes to saying thank you, there are a few things to keep in mind. First, make sure to say it sincerely. Don't just say thank you because it's expected – say it because you truly appreciate what the person has done for you. Second, be specific about what you're thanking them for. Saying "thank you for everything" is nice, but thanking someone for a specific action shows that you've noticed and appreciated what they've done. Finally, take the time to express your gratitude in different ways. Saying thank you in person is great, but sending a handwritten card or email can also be effective.

Now that you know the importance of gratitude and how to say thank you, it's time to start cultivating gratitude in your own life. Here are a few simple exercises to get started:

1. Keep a gratitude journal

Each day, write down three things you're grateful for. They can be big or small – anything that made you feel happy or appreciated that day. Keeping a gratitude journal will help you focus on the positive things in your life, and you can look back on it when you're feeling down.

2. Write thank-you notes

Take some time to write thank-you notes to people who have done something special for you. It could be a family member, friend, co-worker, or anyone else who has made a difference in your life. Sending a handwritten note can make someone's day and reinforce the bond between you.

3. Say thank you more often

Make a conscious effort to say thank you more often in your daily life. Whether it's to a cashier at the grocery store or a colleague at work, acknowledging others' efforts can make them feel appreciated and valued.

In conclusion, cultivating gratitude is a powerful way to improve your life and the lives of those around you. Saying thank you is a simple but effective way to express your gratitude and show appreciation for the people and things in your life. Whether it's through a thank-you note, verbal acknowledgement, or other means, taking the time to say thank you can make a big difference. So start cultivating gratitude today, and see the positive impact it has on your life.

Creating a Cozy Home: Turning Your Space into a Hygge Haven

Do you ever feel like your home is lacking a certain warmth and comfort despite your best efforts? Or do you find yourself constantly feeling stressed or anxious, unable to fully unwind in your own space? If so, it may be time to introduce some hygge into your life.

Hygge is a Danish word that embodies the concept of coziness, contentment, and well-being. It's a way of life that emphasizes simple pleasures, relaxation, and connection with loved ones. And the good news is that you don't have to be Danish or living in Denmark to adopt this lifestyle. Anyone can create a hygge haven in their own home, no matter where they live.

In this chapter, we'll explore some practical tips and examples for creating a cozy and inviting space that promotes relaxation, connection, and joy.

1. Embrace soft lighting
One of the hallmarks of hygge is warm and soft lighting. Harsh overhead lights can be jarring and make it difficult to relax. Instead, opt for lamps with soft and warm bulbs, string lights, or candles to create a cozy ambiance.

For example, you could place a few candles around your living room and switch off the overhead lights in the evening. Or you could string up some fairy lights around your bedroom to create a magical and calming atmosphere.

2. Add texture and warmth
Another way to create a hygge haven is to incorporate a variety of textures and materials throughout your home. Think soft and plush blankets, a fluffy rug, or a cozy armchair. These elements not only add warmth and comfort but also create a sense of visual interest and depth.

For example, you could drape a chunky knit blanket over your sofa or armchair, or invest in some soft and fluffy throw pillows. You could also lay down a plush rug in your bedroom to add some extra warmth and coziness.

3. Create inviting spaces
Hygge is all about connection and togetherness, so it's important to create inviting spaces in your home that encourage socializing and relaxation. This could be a cozy reading nook, a comfortable seating area in your backyard, or a cozy dining room table for family meals.

For example, you could set up a small reading nook in your living room with a comfortable chair, some good books, and a soft blanket. Or you could create a cozy outdoor space with some comfortable chairs, a fire pit, and some string lights. These spaces invite you to slow down, relax and connect with others.

4. Invest in quality, not quantity

Hygge is about celebrating simple pleasures and cherishing what you have. When it comes to creating a hygge haven in your home, it's important to focus on quality over quantity. Invest in a few high-quality and well-made items that you truly love, rather than cluttering your home with cheap and disposable items.

For example, you could invest in a high-quality set of bed linens that feel soft and luxurious to the touch. Or you could invest in a few pieces of handmade pottery or other artisanal pieces for your kitchen or living room.

5. Bring nature indoors

Nature has a calming and restorative effect on the mind and body, so it's important to bring some elements of the natural world into your home. This could be a potted plant, a small herb garden, or a vase of fresh flowers.

For example, you could place a few potted plants around your living room or bedroom to add some greenery and fresh air. Or you could treat yourself to a fresh bouquet of flowers every week to brighten up your space and bring some natural beauty into your home.

Creating a hygge haven in your home doesn't have to be difficult or expensive. By incorporating some of these simple tips and examples, you can transform your space into a warm, inviting, and cozy refuge from the stress and chaos of everyday life. So grab your favorite blanket, light some candles, and get ready to embrace the hygge lifestyle!

Finding Joy in the Outdoors: The Beauty of Nature

As humans, we are natural explorers, always in search of something fascinating and exciting. For many people, the best place to find joy and beauty is in the outdoors, surrounded by nature's many colors and fragrances. There are countless reasons why spending time outdoors is beneficial, but one of the most remarkable is how the natural world encourages relaxation, creativity, and inspiration.

The beauty of nature is a truly magnificent sight. Whether you're watching the sunrise and the sunsets, walking in the woods where the leaves rustle and flutter in a gentle breeze, smelling the perfume of blooming flowers, feeling the warm sand on your feet or enjoying the freshness of an early morning dew, nature never fails to amaze and inspire us.

One of the most striking examples of natural beauty can be observed in the vast and stunning mountains that cover the world. Mountains are one of the most awe-inspiring features of nature, standing tall and majestic amidst the sky. The view of a snow-capped mountain with an alpenglow sunset, seen from a distance, can rival a painting's stunning beauty. Breathing in the crisp mountain air while gazing at the naturally inspired wonder can leave anyone feeling calm and content.

Another of nature's many captivating phenomena is the variety of seasons that occur throughout the year. Each season brings its own unique character and charm, from the rejuvenating spring colors to the warm summer sun, to the enchanting fall foliage, and finally, the enchanting and breathtaking winter landscapes. Whether you prefer to soak up the sun on a summer day, skip through the rustling leaves during the fall, or witness a snow-blanketed winter scenery, the outdoors offers a never-ending display of diverse and captivating scenes.

Even during the warm summer months, the sparkling blue waters in the form of a lake or ocean can offer comfort and calmness. The captivating water levels can provide both adventure and relaxation, from watching the waves crash and listening to the river's sounds to exploring sea caves, snorkeling coral reefs or kayaking with the family.

One of the most enriching experiences of the outdoors is wildlife exposure. Observing both endangered and nondescript animals while still retaining respect for their habitat is a spectacle in itself. Whether it is bird-watching, catching a glimpse of a moose or deer, encountering new creatures while trekking, or merely watching a beautiful butterfly fluttering about, embracing the native species in their environment can be inspiring and thrilling.

Another unique fascination of nature is the vastness of the starry galaxy that exists beyond our planet. Just a little time spent outdoors on a clear, cloudless night can open one's eyes to the universe's endless vastness. From shooting stars to the bright composition of the stars and planets, the truly amazing sight can bring a sense of understanding of one's place and significance within the world.

The beautiful aspect of nature is that everyone can enjoy it differently, whether it is through outdoor activities like trekking, fishing or hunting, observing breathtakingly beautiful sunsets or simply walking through woodland. Given ample opportunities that provide physical and mental well-being, the best part of nature is enjoying it with family and friends. The fun of making s'mores, telling ghost stories or catching a fish with kids fuels the mind and brings simple pleasures of life.

There's no denying that our natural world's beauty and enchantment will shine on forever. As much as we try to capture it on camera, the images are never quite the same as the experience itself. The simple act of finding joy in nature, soaking in the beauty and breathing in the fresh air, can bring a sense of happiness, contentment, and an appreciation for nature that is hard to rival.

All in all, nature is truly priceless. It reminds us of the outstanding beauty that exists within a world that is modernized almost beyond recognition. As much as it may be a cliché, the best things in life are usually the ones that can be embraced and appreciated with intention and purpose. So, next time you are feeling stressed or weighed down, take a break and step outside. Take a deep breath of the fresh outdoors air, bask in the glorious sunshine or the cool breeze, and forget about the worries of the world. The outside world offers one of the most stimulating and calming experiences one can ever imagine, and that is something worth taking the time to experience.

Nourishing Your Body and Soul: Hygge and Self-Care

Hygge is not just about creating a cozy ambiance in your home. It's also about taking the time to care for yourself, both physically and emotionally. In this chapter, we'll explore how you can nourish your body and soul through hygge and self-care.

Body Care:

Taking care of your body is the first step to self-care. When you feel good physically, it reflects on your emotional state. Here are some ways that you can nourish your body:

1. Mindful Eating
Our bodies require proper nutrition to function optimally. The things we eat have a significant impact on our health and wellbeing. Instead of grabbing processed and unhealthy snacks, try to incorporate whole foods into your diet. Start by adding a few fruits and vegetables to your meals. You can also try cooking healthy meals at home, experimenting with new recipes, and purchasing healthier food options.

2. Exercise

Exercise doesn't have to be high-intensity workouts at the gym. You can incorporate small bursts of activity throughout your day, like taking the stairs instead of the elevator or walking during your lunch break. If intense workouts aren't your thing, try low-impact activities like yoga or walking. These exercises promote mental clarity, reduce stress levels, and improve your overall mood.

3. Sleep

Sleep is an essential part of body care. Ensuring that you get enough sleep every night is crucial for your physical wellbeing. A good night's sleep helps in rejuvenating and repairing your body, promotes healthy weight loss, and reduces the risk of health problems like heart disease.

Soul Care:

In addition to physical nourishment, you must take care of your soul as well. Nourishing our souls can manifest in different forms like spending time with loved ones, doing things we love, and practicing spirituality. Here are some ways you can nourish your soul:

1. Mindfulness

Being present in the moment and mindful of your surroundings is an essential practice to nourish your soul. Try to take a moment out of your day to reflect on your thoughts, emotions, and feelings. Meditation and breathing exercises can help in reducing stress, promoting relaxation, and improving your wellbeing.

2. Creativity

Everyone has a creative side, and it's important to let it shine. Engaging in creative activities like painting, drawing, or playing music allows you to express yourself freely and can have a calming and therapeutic effect on your mind and soul.

3. Connection

Connecting with family and friends is vital to nourishing your soul. Even if it's just a phone call or a text message, taking the time to communicate with loved ones can make a significant difference in your mood and wellbeing.

Hygge and Self-Care:

Hygge can be incorporated into your self-care routine and ensure that you are nourishing both your body and soul. Below are some hygge-inspired self-care practices that can help you feel good:

1. Create a cozy home

Creating a welcoming and peaceful environment in your home can have a significant impact on your well-being. Try decorating your space with soft blankets, warm lighting, and soothing scents like candles or essential oils. Curling up with a good book or taking a relaxing bath can also be a great way to unwind and create a peaceful space.

2. Pamper Yourself

Taking time out to pamper yourself is an act of self-care. Try incorporating a weekly self-care ritual like a bath or a facial to your routine. You can also try making your own products like body oils or face masks using natural ingredients.

3. Disconnect

In today's world, it's easy to get caught up in the hustle and bustle of our daily lives. Take some time each day to unplug and disconnect from technology. This can help you feel more centered and focused on the present moment.

In conclusion, nourishing your body and soul through hygge and self-care is essential for your overall wellbeing. Incorporating these practices into your daily routine can have a significant impact on your mood, energy levels, and overall health. Remember to take care of yourself both physically and emotionally, and create a warm and cozy environment that contributes to your well-being. By taking time out to care for yourself, you'll be more capable of fulfilling your goals and living a happy and fulfilling life.

Hygge in Relationships: Connecting with Others in a Meaningful Way

Connection is a fundamental aspect of human life, and it stands at the core of every long-lasting relationship. In a world that seems to be constantly on the move, we are often in a rush to get things done and forget to take the time to connect with the people around us. This is where Hygge comes in. Hygge is a Danish concept that translates to a cozy, comfortable feeling, and it relies on the idea of creating a warm atmosphere to connect authentically with others in a meaningful way.

Hygge can be applied to relationships in various forms. While it can be used to build new relationships, it can also help deepen existing ones. In Hygge, relationships are not just about the physical aspects of being together. It's about creating an emotional bond and feeling comfortable in each other's company.

One of the essential elements of Hygge is slowing down and taking the time to connect with the people important to you. For instance, you can set aside some time to sit with your loved ones and catch up on how they're doing, without being too focused on other distractions around you. It could be in the form of going out to dinner, sitting by the fireplace, or just spending the evening at home playing a board game.

Hygge also involves creating an atmosphere of trust, safety, and warmth, where people can be themselves without fear of judgment. It's a feeling of belonging that comes with being in the company of those who value you for who you are. For instance, you may put some fresh flowers on the table, light some candles, and listen to soft ambient music to help create an environment that promotes calmness and relaxation. This way, everyone can feel at home and truly connected.

Sharing food is another essential aspect of Hygge in relationships. Sharing a meal with loved ones is one of the most fundamental ways to create a sense of togetherness. It doesn't have to be anything fancy; it could be something as simple as cooking a homemade meal or enjoying a cup of coffee. Eating together encourages bonding and helps create an environment for people to open up and share their feelings.

Incorporating Hygge in your relationships can help you build a deeper sense of intimacy with your partner. For example, taking a relaxing bath together, or cuddling up under a blanket while watching a movie promotes relaxation and helps remove any distractions that may interfere with the connection. It's a great way to slow down and connect with your partner on a deeper level.

Hygge can also be applied to building relationships with your friends. Meeting up for a cup of coffee or going for a walk together provides opportunities to connect in a meaningful way. It creates an environment that encourages laughter, connection, and acceptance.

Hygge also reminds us to appreciate the moment, to be mindful of the people in front of us, and to appreciate the little things that make our lives better. For instance, you may take a moment to appreciate the warmth of the sun on your skin, or the sound of the birds chirping in the morning. These little things help us connect with the present moment, encouraging us to enjoy every moment with the people around us.

Hygge in relationships not only helps build deeper connections but also promotes a sense of emotional wellbeing. By engaging in simple activities like reading a book, taking a walk or cooking together, we feel respected, valued, and loved. It puts us in a relaxed mental state that allows us to enjoy our life and relationships better.

In conclusion, Hygge in relationships is about creating a comfortable, safe, and calming atmosphere that promotes connection and authenticity. It encourages us to slow down, be present, and appreciate the people around us. Hygge provides an opportunity to cultivate relationships, deepen existing ones, and create an environment that promotes happiness, understanding, and togetherness. Try incorporating Hygge into your relationships and see how it changes for the better.

Mindful Technology Use: Balancing Screen Time with Hygge Moments

It's no secret that technology has drastically changed the way we live our lives. From smartphones that allow us to have the world at our fingertips, to streaming services that let us consume limitless entertainment, technology has made our lives easier and more convenient than ever before. However, with this convenience comes a downside. Many of us are spending too much time glued to our screens, which can have some adverse effects on our mental health and overall well-being.

Fortunately, there is an easy way to counteract the negative effects of technology without giving it up entirely: hygge moments. Hygge (pronounced "hoo-gah") is a Danish term for taking pleasure in life's simple pleasures and cultivating a sense of coziness and contentment. By incorporating hygge moments into our daily lives, we can find a sense of balance between our technology use and our need for relaxation and enjoyment.

One of the biggest impacts technology has had on our lives is on our sleep. With the constant availability of screens, it's easy to stay up late scrolling through social media or binge-watching our favorite shows. However, this type of screen time can negatively affect our quality of sleep, leaving us feeling groggy and unrefreshed in the morning.

To combat this, try incorporating some hygge moments into your bedtime routine. Instead of scrolling through your phone, try reading a book or taking a warm bath. Create a comfortable and relaxing environment by using soft lighting, cozy blankets, and soothing music. By taking the time to unwind before bed, you'll be able to get a better night's sleep, which will make you feel more energized and alert the next day.

Another area where technology can have a negative impact on our lives is on our social connections. While social media platforms have made it easier than ever to stay connected with friends and family, they can also lead to feelings of isolation and disconnection. When we spend too much time scrolling through social media feeds, we may feel like we're keeping up with our loved ones, but in reality, we're missing out on the meaningful connections that come from face-to-face interactions.

To combat this, try incorporating some hygge moments into your social interactions. Instead of scrolling through Instagram while hanging out with friends, try having a game night or cooking dinner together. Instead of texting your significant other, try writing them a love letter or planning a special date night. By being present and intentional with how we spend our time with loved ones, we can cultivate deeper and more meaningful connections that technology can't replicate.

Lastly, technology can also have a negative impact on how we feel about ourselves. With the constant bombardment of perfect bodies, perfect vacations, and perfect lives on social media, it's easy to feel like we're not measuring up. This can lead to feelings of self-doubt and low self-esteem, which can have a significant impact on our mental health.

To combat this, try incorporating some hygge moments into your self-care routine. Instead of obsessively checking your phone for likes and comments, try practicing some self-care activities that make you feel good. This could be anything from taking a yoga class to going for a hike in nature. By taking the time to care for ourselves and focus on our own well-being, we can cultivate a sense of self-love and confidence that can't be found online.

Incorporating hygge moments into our daily lives may seem simple, but it can have a significant impact on our overall well-being. By being mindful of how we spend our time with technology and intentionally incorporating some cozy and calming moments into our daily routines, we can find balance, peace, and contentment in our lives.

For example, say you've had a long day at work and you're feeling stressed and overwhelmed. Instead of reaching for your phone and scrolling through social media, try taking a few minutes to practice some mindfulness activities. This could be anything from practicing deep breathing to taking a relaxing bath. By being present in the moment and practicing mindfulness, you'll be able to reduce your stress levels and feel more calm and centered.

Another example could be when you're feeling bored or restless and are tempted to mindlessly scroll through your phone. Instead, try taking a break and practicing some self-care activities. This could be anything from taking a relaxing walk in nature to cooking or baking something delicious. By taking the time to care for yourself and engage in activities that bring you joy, you'll be able to cultivate a sense of happiness and contentment that's much more fulfilling than anything you can find online.

In conclusion, by balancing our screen time with hygge moments, we can find a sense of balance, peace, and contentment in our lives. By being mindful of how we spend our time with technology and intentionally incorporating some cozy, calming, and meaningful moments into our daily routines, we can cultivate a deeper sense of well-being and happiness that can't be found online. So go ahead and curl up with a good book, light a candle, and savor the goodness of a hygge moment – your mind and body will thank you for it!

Creating a Hygge Community: Spreading Comfort and Joy to Others

Hygge isn't just about making yourself feel good. It's also about spreading that feeling to others, creating a community of comfort and joy that can be felt by everyone around you. Here are some tips for creating a hygge community and spreading comfort and joy to others.

Create a Welcoming Atmosphere

One of the first steps in creating a hygge community is to create a welcoming atmosphere. This means taking the time to create a space that feels warm, cozy, and inviting. Whether you're welcoming friends and family into your home or simply interacting with people throughout your day, creating a welcoming atmosphere can help put people at ease and make them feel more comfortable.

Some ways to create a welcoming atmosphere might include setting up comfortable seating areas, creating a warm and inviting color scheme, and filling your space with soft lighting and candles. You might also consider setting out a few comfort items like blankets or pillows to encourage people to relax and unwind.

Connect Through Shared Experiences

Another way to spread comfort and joy in your community is to connect with others through shared experiences. This might mean hosting a get-together with friends or family, attending a community event, or simply spending time with the people around you.

By connecting with others through shared experiences, you can create a sense of camaraderie and togetherness that can be incredibly comforting. This might mean planning a regular game night with friends, attending a local community event like a farmer's market or street fair, or simply going for a walk with a friend.

Offer Comfort and Support

Sometimes spreading comfort and joy can mean offering comfort and support to those around you. This might mean lending an ear when someone needs to talk, providing a warm meal or cup of tea to someone who's had a difficult day, or simply offering a comforting hug when someone needs it most.

Offering comfort and support to those around you can help to create a sense of closeness and community, and can also help to alleviate stress and anxiety in those who might be dealing with difficult times.

Celebrate Simple Pleasures

Another key aspect of hygge is celebrating the simple pleasures in life. This might mean enjoying a warm cup of tea on a cool evening, taking a leisurely walk through the park, or simply savoring a delicious meal with friends and family.

By celebrating the simple pleasures in life, we can often find comfort and joy in the everyday moments that might otherwise pass us by. This might mean going out of our way to notice the beautiful sunset or sunrise, appreciating the changing colors of the leaves in the fall, or simply taking a moment to appreciate the beauty of a loved one's smile.

Practice Gratitude and Mindfulness

Finally, one of the most important aspects of creating a hygge community is to practice gratitude and mindfulness. This means taking the time to appreciate the good things in life and to savor the moments that bring us joy and comfort.

By practicing gratitude and mindfulness, we can become more attuned to the simple pleasures in life and more open to the connections and experiences around us. This might mean taking a few deep breaths before a meal to appreciate the company and the food, or simply taking a moment to express gratitude for the people and experiences in our lives.

Creating a hygge community isn't about grand gestures or expensive gifts. It's about creating a warm, comfortable atmosphere where people can come together to share experiences, connect with others, and spread comfort and joy in their daily lives. Whether it's hosting a cozy get-together with friends or simply taking a few deep breaths before a meal, there are countless ways to infuse your life with the warmth and goodness of hygge.

Thankful Reflections: Discovering the Serenity of Hygge

As I sit here writing the final words of my book, I cannot help but feel grateful for this journey. Writing this book has been a labor of love, and I couldn't have done it without the support of my three young daughters and my loving husband. They have been my constant source of inspiration and the driving force behind my passion for helping others find happiness, comfort, and joy in their lives.

Throughout this book, I have shared with you the concepts and practices of Hygge, the Danish term for creating a cozy and comfortable atmosphere to promote well-being and happiness. I have provided you with practical tips, simple exercises, and easy-to-follow advice to help you infuse Hygge into your everyday life.

But the most important thing that I hope you take away from this book is that finding comfort and joy is within your grasp. You don't need to wait for the perfect moment, the ideal setting or material possessions to achieve it. You already have everything you need within you. By embracing the simple pleasures of life, cultivating meaningful relationships, and savoring the present moment, you can unlock the power of Hygge and experience genuine happiness and well-being.

As I conclude this book, I want to express my heartfelt gratitude to you, the reader. Thank you for taking the time and effort to read this book, and for allowing me to share my thoughts and experiences with you. It has been my hope that my words have provided you with a sense of comfort, guidance, and inspiration in your pursuit of a more fulfilling life.

In closing, let me offer you my sincere best wishes for your journey ahead. Remember that finding comfort and joy is a lifelong process, and that there are no shortcuts to true happiness. But by following the principles of Hygge, you can create the conditions for happiness and well-being in your life. So, take care, be kind to yourself, and always stay open to the wonders that life has to offer.

Thank you once again, and all the very best to you.

With gratitude,
Maria Johanson

Hygge affirmations

1. I am deserving of comfort and coziness.
2. I am grateful for the little moments of joy in my life.
3. I embrace warmth and tranquility in my surroundings.
4. I am at peace with myself and my environment.
5. I invite calmness and relaxation into my daily routine.
6. I appreciate the simple pleasures in life.
7. I focus on the present and the beauty around me.
8. I am content with who I am and where I am in life.
9. I find happiness in the small, meaningful moments.
10. I prioritize self-care and well-being.
11. I find comfort in the company of loved ones.
12. I am mindful and present in my interactions with others.
13. I take time to unwind and recharge my energy.
14. I embrace the imperfections and quirks of life.
15. I celebrate the unique qualities that make me who I am.
16. I am surrounded by love and positivity.
17. I am open to new experiences and possibilities.
18. I find happiness in slowing down and savoring the moment.
19. I am grateful for the abundance of riches in my life.
20. I am content with a simple and uncomplicated lifestyle.
21. I appreciate the beauty in nature and the outdoors.
22. I am at peace with myself and my past experiences.
23. I prioritize rest and relaxation to nourish my mind and body.

24. I choose to see the good in people and situations.

25. I am grateful for the warmth and comfort of my home.

26. I choose to live with intention and purpose.

27. I embrace a slower pace of life, free from stress and anxiety.

28. I am surrounded by joy and positivity.

29. I am mindful of the beauty and wonder in each day.

30. I find peace in the stillness of my surroundings.

31. I am kind and compassionate towards myself and others.

32. I appreciate the beauty in simplicity.

33. I am grateful for the love and support of those around me.

34. I make time for the things that bring me joy and happiness.

35. I am present and mindful in every moment.

36. I prioritize relationships and meaningful connections.

37. I allow myself to feel all emotions and embrace them fully.

38. I am content with what I have and who I am.

39. I choose to live a life of purpose and meaning.

40. I am surrounded by beauty and tranquility.

41. I find pleasure in the small and ordinary moments of life.

42. I choose to focus on the positive and let go of negativity.

43. I am grateful for the blessings in my life, big and small.

44. I am at peace with the uncertainty of life.

45. I am surrounded by love and positivity.

46. I prioritize self-reflection and personal growth.

47. I find beauty in the imperfections of life.

48. I am content with the slow and steady pace of progress.

49. I appreciate the small acts of kindness that make a difference.

50. I am deserving of a life filled with warmth, joy, and contentment.

A list of books to read for a cozy feeling

1. The Guernsey Literary and Potato Peel Pie Society by Mary Ann Shaffer and Annie Barrows
2. The Nightingale by Kristin Hannah
3. Little Women by Louisa May Alcott
4. Anne of Green Gables by L.M. Montgomery
5. The Secret Garden by Frances Hodgson Burnett
6. Where the Crawdads Sing by Delia Owens
7. A Man Called Ove by Fredrik Backman
8. The Bookish Life of Nina Hill by Abbi Waxman
9. Pride and Prejudice by Jane Austen
10. The Time Keeper by Mitch Albom
11. The Christmas Shoes by Donna VanLiere
12. The Little Paris Bookshop by Nina George
13. The Cozy Life: Rediscover the Joy of the Simple Things Through the Danish Concept of Hygge by Pia Edberg (non-fiction)
14. The Cottage on Sunshine Beach by Holly Martin
15. The Rosie Project by Graeme Simsion.

Lexicon of hygge related words

1. Hygge - (pronounced "hoo-guh"): A feeling of warmth, coziness, and joy.

2. Hyggelig - The adjective form of hygge, meaning cozy, warm, and inviting.

3. Kos - The Swedish word for hygge, meaning the same thing: coziness and comfort.

4. Gemütlichkeit - The German equivalent of hygge, translating to coziness.

5. Fika - The Swedish tradition of taking a break to enjoy a hot drink and a sweet treat with friends.

6. Lagom - The Swedish concept of moderation and balance, a key component of a hygge lifestyle.

7. Julehygge - The Danish word for Christmas hygge, meaning a festive and cozy time spent with loved ones.

8. Smørrebrød - The Danish tradition of open-faced sandwiches, often eaten in cozy cafes on a cold day.

9. Lørdagshygge - The Danish weekend tradition of spending time with family and friends, cooking good food, and relaxing together.

10. Dansk design - The Danish design aesthetic known for its sleek and cozy style, often used to create a hygge atmosphere.

11. Lagomliv - The Swedish word for a balanced life, often encouraging a simple and cozy lifestyle.

12. Kanelbullar - The Swedish tradition of baking cinnamon rolls, bringing warmth and comfort to the home.

13. Kaffepaus - The Swedish tradition of taking a coffee break in the middle of the workday to recharge and relax.

14. Saunassa - The Finnish tradition of spending time in a sauna, promoting relaxation and warmth.

15. Heimattreue - The German word for feeling at home, often linked to a sense of comfort and coziness.

16. Gula katter - The Swedish term for cozy, "yellow cats" - those who love warmth and comfort.

17. Tonttu - The Finnish word for an elf-like creature that brings warmth and joy to the home, often associated with the hygge lifestyle.

18. Glögg - The Swedish and Danish tradition of drinking warm, spiced wine during the winter months.

19. Nisse - The Danish and Norwegian version of the tonttu, a kind-hearted elf who spreads joy and comfort.

20. Sisu - A Finnish concept of strength, resilience, and persistence, often used to create a positive mindset toward a hygge lifestyle.

21. Lys - The Danish tradition of lighting candles to create a cozy and warm atmosphere.

22. Sankthansaften - The Danish tradition of celebrating midsummer with bonfires and outdoor activities.

23. Kaamos - The Finnish word for the darkness of winter, often associated with the need for a cozy and warm atmosphere.

24. Kakslauttanen - A Finnish hotel made famous for its cozy glass igloos that provide a hygge experience while staying warm in the winter outdoors.

25. Kutsu - The Finnish term for hospitality and welcoming guests into the home, a key component of the hygge lifestyle.

Milton Keynes UK
Ingram Content Group UK Ltd.
UKHW020727120224
437701UK00018B/687

9 798223 308850